100 EASY CHECKMATES

1- AND 2-MOVE CHECKMATES TO CHALLENGE YOUR SKILL

100EASY
CHECKMATES

1- AND 2-MOVE CHECKMATES TO CHALLENGE YOUR SKILL

LARRY EVANS

CARDOZA PUBLISHING

Cardoza Publishing is the foremost gaming publisher in the world, with a library of over 200 up-to-date and easy-to-read books and strategies. These authoritative works are written by the top experts in their fields and with more than 10,000,000 books in print, represent the best-selling and most popular gaming books anywhere.

Library of Congress Control Number: 2017955759
ISBN: 978-1-58042-355-7

Visit our web site—www.cardozabooks.com—or write for a full list of books and computer strategies.

CARDOZA PUBLISHING
P.O. Box 98115, Las Vegas, NV 89193
Phone (800) 577-WINS
email: cardozabooks@aol.com

ABOUT THE AUTHOR

Grandmaster Larry Evans, one of America's most celebrated chess authorities, is a 5-time USA champion and author of more than twenty chess books including *New Ideas in Chess*, *10 Most Common Chess Mistakes*, 200 *Chess Endgame Solutions*, and his collaboration on Bobby Fischer's classic *My 60 Memorable Games*. He was a long-time contributor to *Chess Life*, and his syndicated chess column, "Evans on Chess," had appeared continuously for almost 40 years. Evans has beaten or drawn games against six world champions: Euwe, Karpov, Petrosian, Spassky, Smyslov, and Fischer, as well as dozens of the world's top players.

Evans first won the Marshall Club Championship at age fifteen and the New York State Championship at age sixteen. He won the USA Closed Championship five times (the first time in 1951, the last time in 1980—a remarkable span), the USA Open four times, the 1956 Canadian Open, and had numerous wins at many other opens including first place at an international tournament in Portugal in 1974. Evans represented the USA on eight Olympic teams (including the gold medal team in 1976) and served as captain in 1982. Evans was the youngest player to capture the nation's highest chess title at age nineteen, a record surpassed by Bobby Fischer at age fourteen. He is sometimes referred to as "the Dean of American Chess."

TABLE OF CONTENTS

1

INTRODUCTION

"Chess is a mind game, the objective of which is to checkmate or kill the opposing king. Ultimately that is the only way to win, unless an opponent, staring inevitable defeat in the face, voluntarily opts to resign. It is no surprise that throughout the ages chess has attracted both political and military leaders, including Queen Elizabeth I, her father, Henry VIII, the Russian czars, Ivan the Terrible, Peter the Great and Napoleon."

— British grandmaster Raymond Keene

The word checkmate derives from the Persian *shah* (meaning "king") and *mat* (meaning "dead"). Thus, the king is dead. But his majesty is never actually captured because one side wins if and when the opposing king is attacked but has no legal escape.

The purpose of this book is to teach beginners how to use 100 basic patterns for achieving checkmate. All the positions I show here are from real tournament games that took place after 2000. Most losers resigned a few moves before they saw mate coming. In the 19th century, however, many players fought to the bitter end.

The Basics of Chess Notation

Before we begin looking at the checkmates, it's important that you have a basic familiarity with chess notation, a simple way of recording moves in a chess game. Chess notation starts with looking at the chess board as a coordinate grid. Take a look at the diagram below.

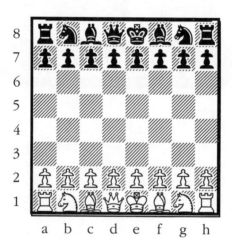

The horizontal rows, called ranks, are numbered from 1 to 8. White's first row is always number 1, which makes Black's back row number 8. The vertical rows, called files, are lettered from a to h. They go from left to right (looking from White's perspective).With this grid system, we can refer to any square on the board by name. For example, White's queen is now on d1. Black has a bishop on f8. When you become a more advanced chess player, you will also learn how to record moves using chess notation. For the purposes of this book, though, I will write each move in plain English to ensure that you fully understand what's happening at all times.

2

BASIC MATING EXAMPLES

The Fool's Mate

A fool's mate does not refer to a chessplayer's spouse. It's simply the quickest way to win, and it requires just two moves. Take a look at the diagrams below.

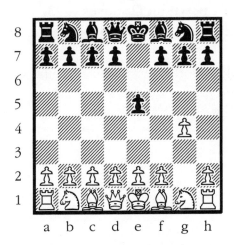

1. White's pawn on g2 moves to g4.
    Black's pawn on e7 moves to e5.

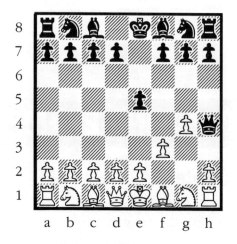

2.   White's pawn on f2 moves to f3.
       Black's queen moves to h4 for checkmate.

The Fool's Mate works only because White erred so badly
in the opening.

BASIC MATING EXAMPLES

The Scholar's Mate

Another popular trap that might work for you a few times is called the Scholar's Mate. It requires four moves:

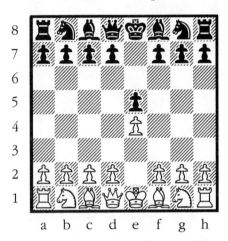

1. White's pawn on e2 moves to e4.
   Black's pawn on e7 moves to e5.

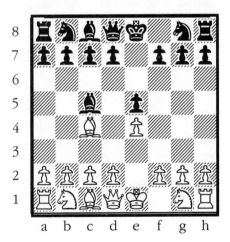

2. White's bishop on f1 moves to c4.
   Black's bishop on f8 moves to c5.

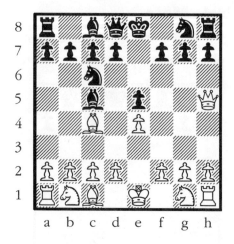

3.   White's queen moves to h5.
     Black's knight on b8 moves to c6.

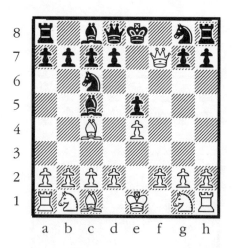

4.   White's queen moves to f7 for checkmate.

Notice that Black can easily thwart the Scholar's Mate if, on the third move, he instead moves his queen to e7.

BASIC MATING EXAMPLES

Mates by Castling

Possibly the earliest example of mate by castling took place in New Orleans in 1854. Paul Morphy, a 17-year-old, used castling to defeat his father, Alonzo Morphy, in the following situation:

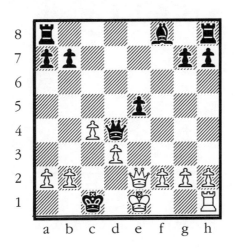

White mates in one move!

The solution is for White to castle (king moves to g1 and rook there crosses over it to f1), and the Black king has no way out.

Another example of mate by castling could have occurred in a famous game between Edward Lasker and G.A. Thomas at the London Chess Club in 1912.

White mates in one move, in two possible ways.

Lasker chose to move his king to d2, yet castling queenside would also do the trick. Which method do you find more pleasing?

BASIC MATING EXAMPLES

A Veteran's Error

If you imagine that veterans are immune to overlooking simple mates even with plenty of time on their clocks in serious tournaments, then consider this sample.

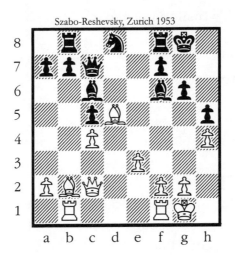

Szabo-Reshevsky, Zurich 1953

White mates in two moves.

Szabo actually moved his bishop from b2 to capture the bishop on f6 (in error) and the game was later drawn. He missed a win by pin with:

1. **White's queen captures the pawn on g6 for check.** (The queen can't be taken because it's illegal to expose the king to capture from the bishop on d5; thus the pawn on f7 is said to be pinned).

Black's king goes to h8.

2. White's bishop on b2 takes Black's bishop on f6 for checkmate.

or...

1.   White's queen captures the pawn on g6 for check.

Black's bishop goes to g7.

2.   White's queen takes the bishop on g7 for checkmate.

"One does not look for a mate in two against a grandmaster," explained Szabo.

Summary

Although the goal is to checkmate the enemy king, don't expect an early knockout. You must conduct your attack methodically, and often fuel it with sacrifice of material to expose the enemy king.

The next chapters contain 100 more examples of situations in which checkmate is possible in just a few moves. The answers are available at the end of the book, but see if you can solve all of these yourself. Early diagrams are easier than the later ones, but you should have little trouble solving them all as you gain experience along the way.

Go to it!

3

MATES IN ONE MOVE

See if you can solve this first group of diagrams. In each one, White should be able to achieve checkmate in just one move.

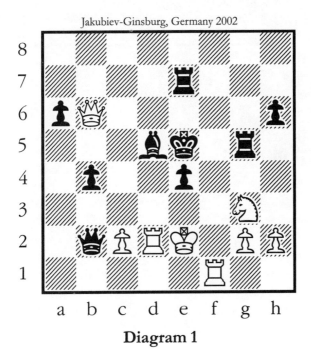

Jakubiev-Ginsburg, Germany 2002

Diagram 1

Your Solution:

Karadiniz-DeFirmian, Bled Olympiad 2002

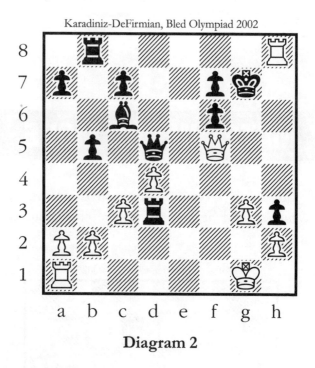

Diagram 2

Your Solution:

MATES IN ONE MOVE

Mudongo-Nanteza, United Arab Emirates 2001

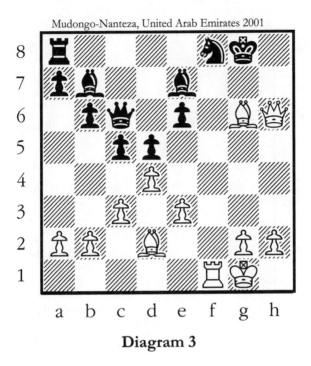

Diagram 3

Your Solution:

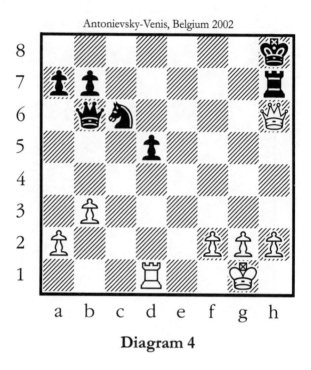

Antonievsky-Venis, Belgium 2002

Diagram 4

Your Solution:

MATES IN ONE MOVE

Adams-Ponomariov, Linares 2002

Diagram 5

Your Solution:

Banas-Cibulkia, Slovakia 2002

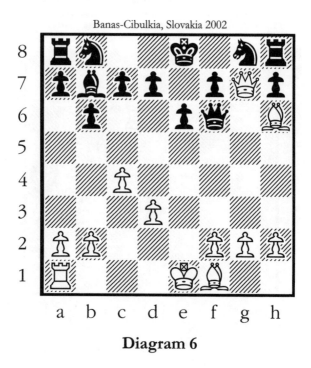

Diagram 6

Your Solution:

MATES IN ONE MOVE

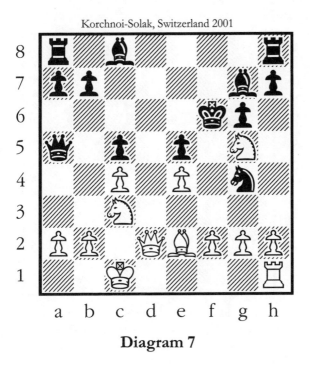

Korchnoi-Solak, Switzerland 2001

Diagram 7

Your Solution:

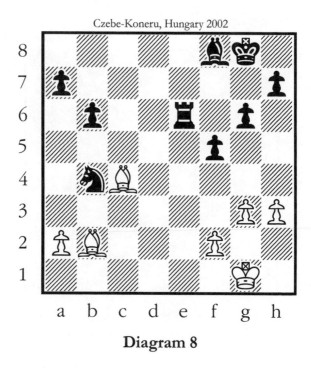

Czebe-Koneru, Hungary 2002

Diagram 8

Your Solution:

Flores-Fiorito, Argentina 2002

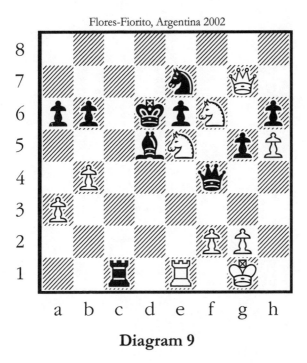

Diagram 9

Your Solution:

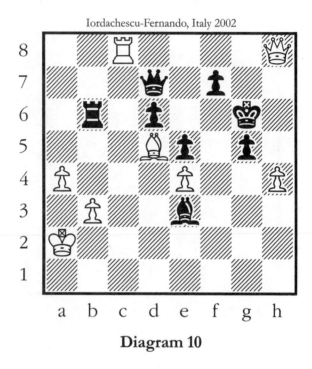

Iordachescu-Fernando, Italy 2002

Diagram 10

Your Solution: (look for two ways)

MATES IN ONE MOVE

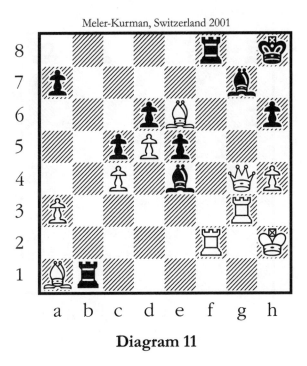

Meler-Kurman, Switzerland 2001

Diagram 11

Your Solution:

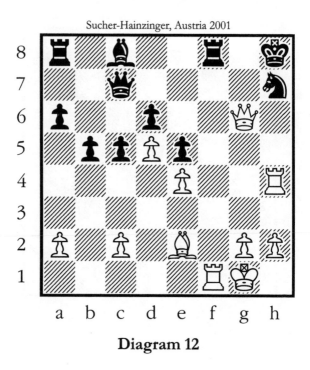

Sucher-Hainzinger, Austria 2001

Diagram 12

Your Solution:

MATES IN ONE MOVE

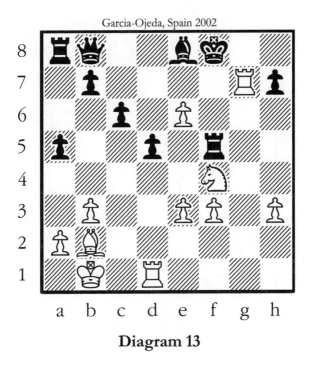

Garcia-Ojeda, Spain 2002

Diagram 13

Your Solution:

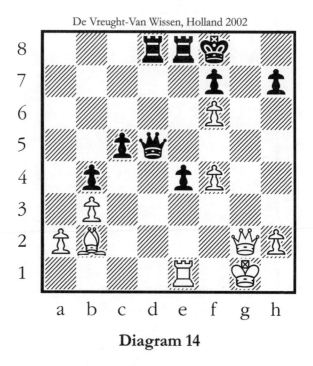

De Vreught-Van Wissen, Holland 2002

Diagram 14

Your Solution:

MATES IN ONE MOVE

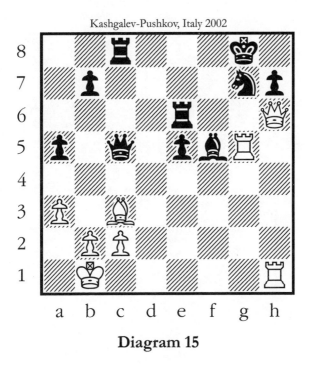

Kashgalev-Pushkov, Italy 2002

Diagram 15

Your Solution:

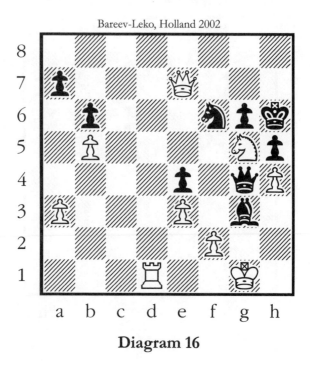

Bareev-Leko, Holland 2002

Diagram 16

Your Solution:

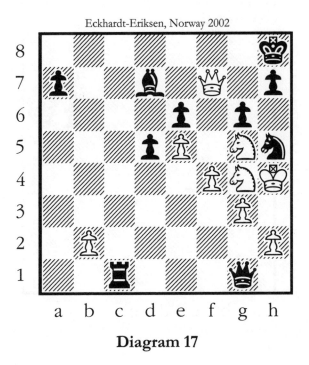

Eckhardt-Eriksen, Norway 2002

Diagram 17

Your Solution: (look for two ways)

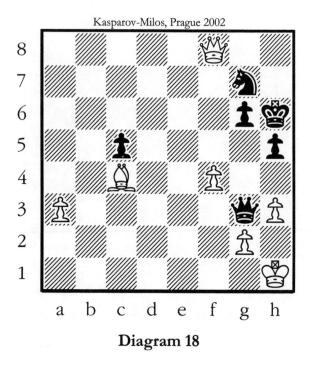

Kasparov-Milos, Prague 2002

Diagram 18

Your Solution:

MATES IN ONE MOVE

Tchadejev-Papin, Under 14 world championship 2002

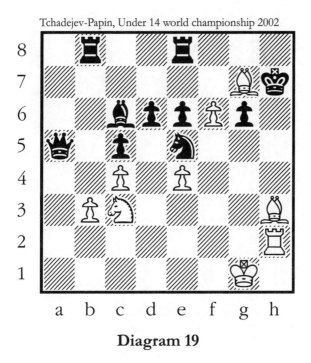

Diagram 19

Your Solution:

Konguvel-Pour, India 2002

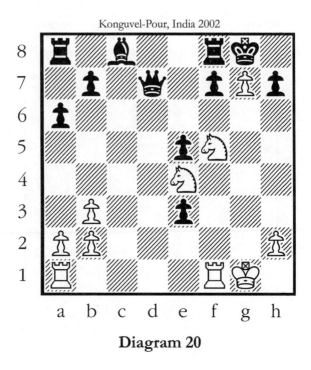

Diagram 20

Your Solution:

MATES IN ONE MOVE

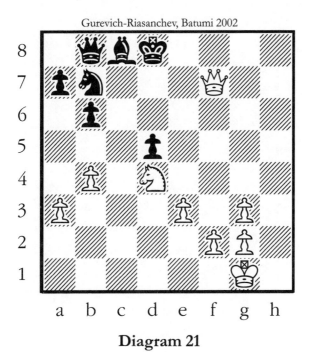

Gurevich-Riasanchev, Batumi 2002

Diagram 21

Your Solution:

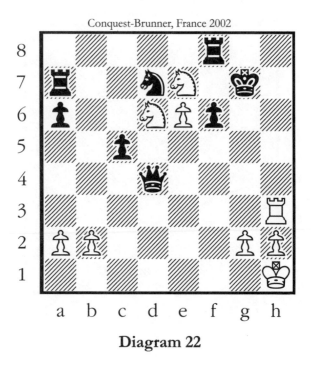

Conquest-Brunner, France 2002

Diagram 22

Your Solution:

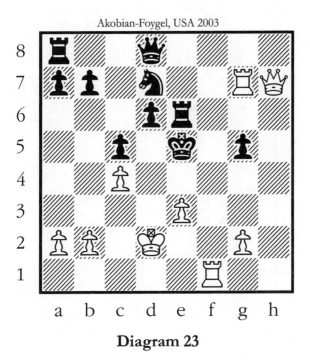

Akobian-Foygel, USA 2003

Diagram 23

Your Solution:

Vijayalakshmi-Swathi, India 2001

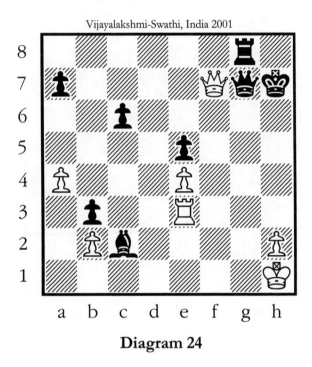

Diagram 24

Your Solution:

MATES IN ONE MOVE

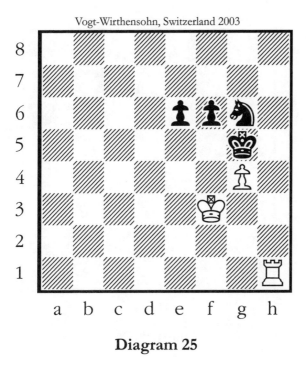

Vogt-Wirthensohn, Switzerland 2003

Diagram 25

Your Solution:

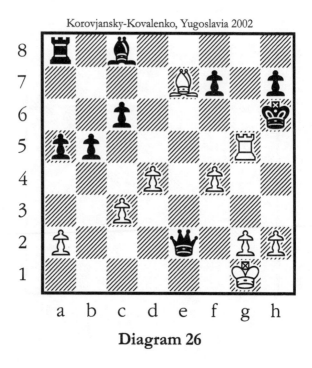

Korovjansky-Kovalenko, Yugoslavia 2002

Diagram 26

Your Solution:

MATES IN ONE MOVE

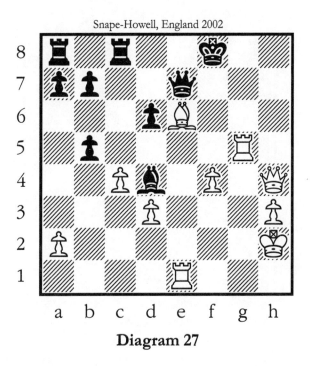

Snape-Howell, England 2002

Diagram 27

Your Solution:

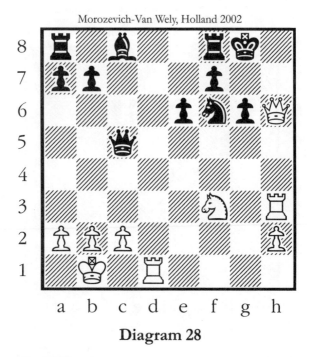

Morozevich-Van Wely, Holland 2002

Diagram 28

Your Solution:

MATES IN ONE MOVE

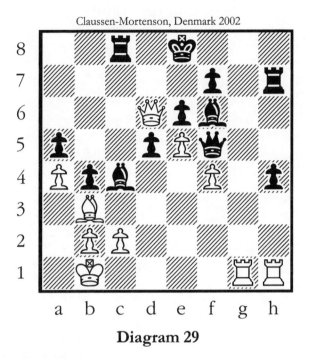

Claussen-Mortenson, Denmark 2002

Diagram 29

Your Solution:

4

MATES IN TWO MOVES

Let's make your task just a little bit harder. In each of the next group of diagrams, White should be able to achieve checkmate in just two moves.

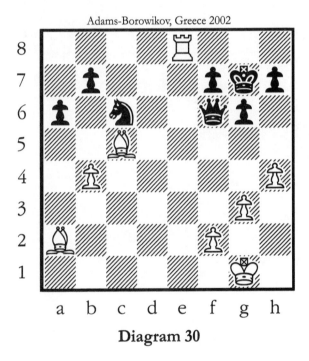

Adams-Borowikov, Greece 2002

Diagram 30

Your Solution:

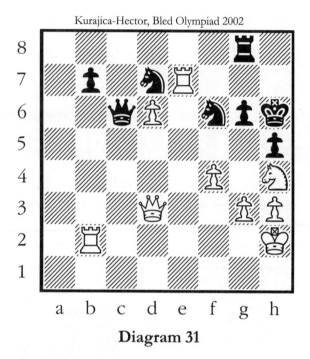

Kurajica-Hector, Bled Olympiad 2002

Diagram 31

Your Solution:

MATES IN TWO MOVES

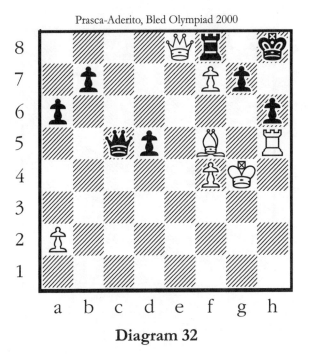

Prasca-Aderito, Bled Olympiad 2000

Diagram 32

Your Solution:

Grigore-Nita, Romania 2002

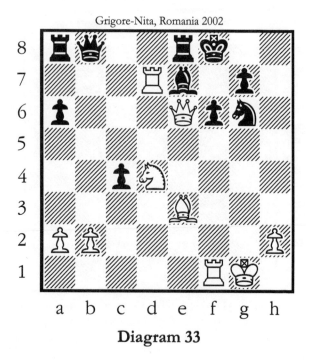

Diagram 33

Your Solution:

Lupulescu-Markov, Spain 2002

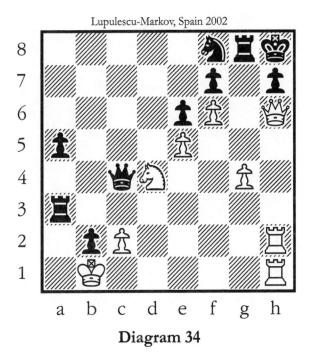

Diagram 34

Your Solution:

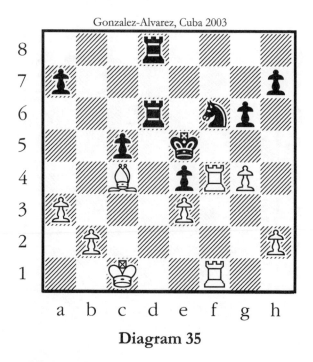

Gonzalez-Alvarez, Cuba 2003

Diagram 35

Your Solution:

MATES IN TWO MOVES

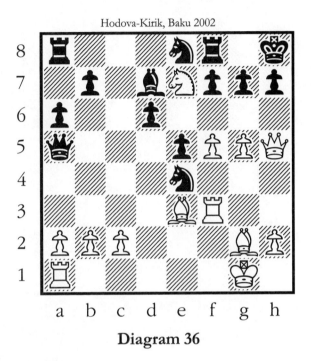

Hodova-Kirik, Baku 2002

Diagram 36

Your Solution:

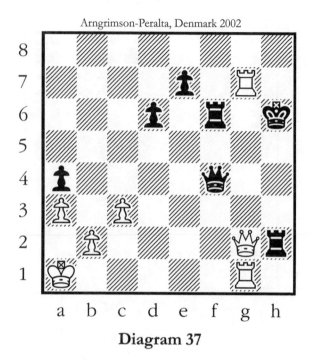

Arngrimson-Peralta, Denmark 2002

Diagram 37

Your Solution:

MATES IN TWO MOVES

Paul-Padilla, USA 2002

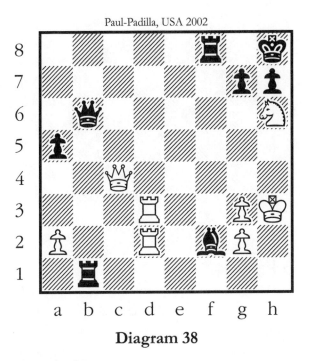

Diagram 38

Your Solution:

Zimbeck-Gold, USA 2000

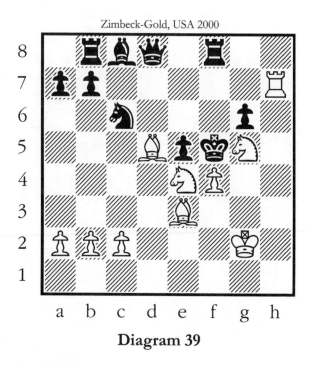

Diagram 39

Your Solution:

MATES IN TWO MOVES

Guidarelli-Ruck, Bled Olympiad 2002

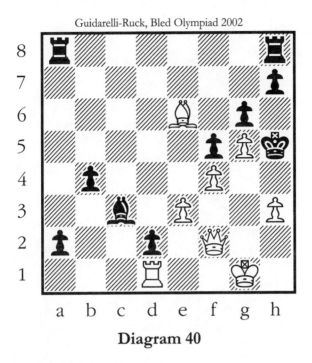

Diagram 40

Your Solution: (look for two ways)

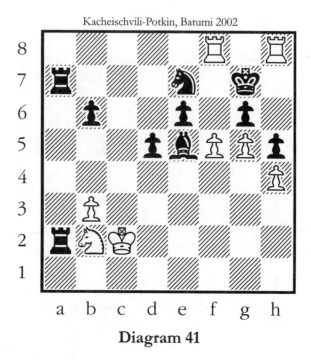

Kacheischvili-Potkin, Batumi 2002

Diagram 41

Your Solution:

MATES IN TWO MOVES

Christ-Berezovsky, Germany 2001

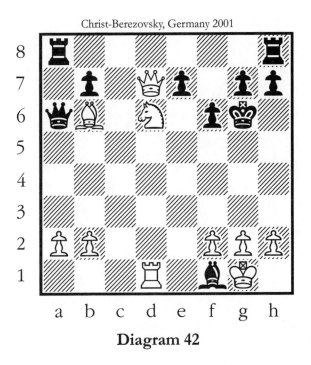

Diagram 42

Your Solution: (look for two ways)

Owod-Thorfinsson, Budapest 2002

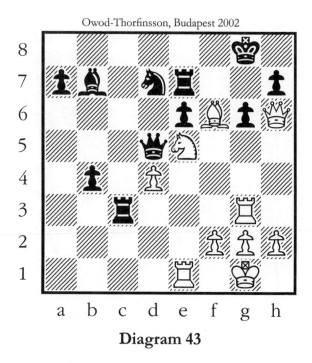

Diagram 43

Your Solution:

MATES IN TWO MOVES

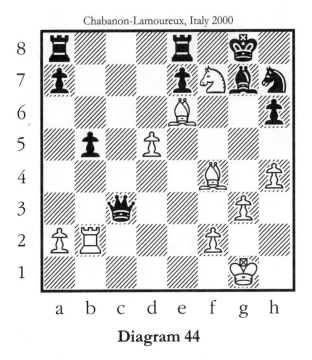

Chabanon-Lamoureux, Italy 2000

Diagram 44

Your Solution:

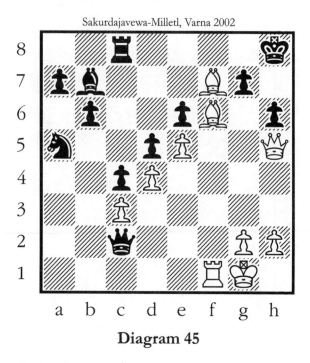

Sakurdajavewa-Milletl, Varna 2002

Diagram 45

Your Solution:

Matwejewa-Repkova, Varna 2002

Diagram 46

Your Solution:

Czarnota-Tomczak, Poland 2002

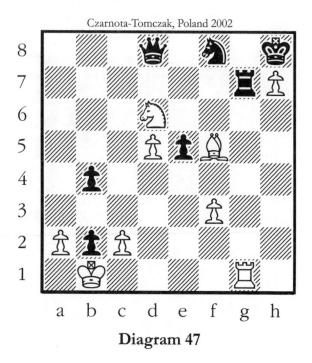

Diagram 47

Your Solution:

MATES IN TWO MOVES

Biolet-Trapl, Czech Championship 2002

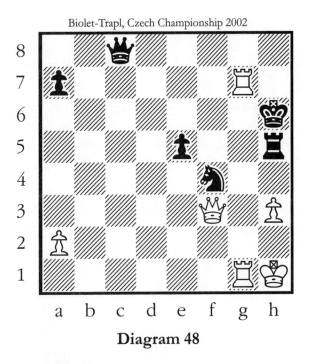

Diagram 48

Your Solution: (look for two ways)

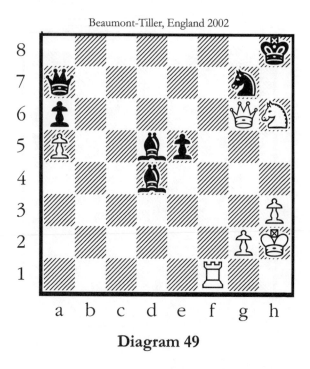

Beaumont-Tiller, England 2002

Diagram 49

Your Solution:

MATES IN TWO MOVES

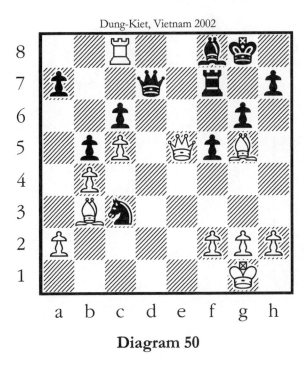

Dung-Kiet, Vietnam 2002

Diagram 50

Your Solution:

Paschall-Rouleau, USA 2002

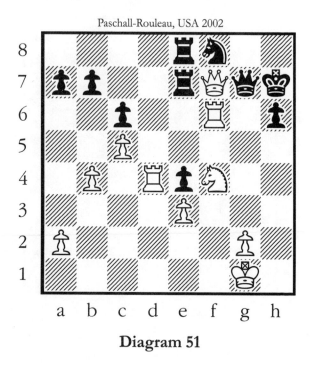

Diagram 51

Your Solution:

MATES IN TWO MOVES

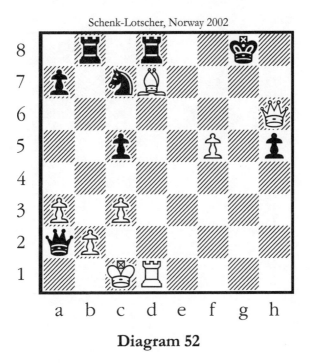

Schenk-Lotscher, Norway 2002

Diagram 52

Your Solution:

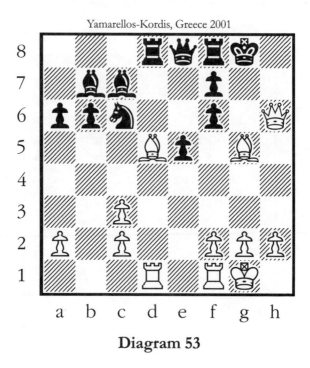

Yamarellos-Kordis, Greece 2001

Diagram 53

Your Solution: (look for two ways)

MATES IN TWO MOVES

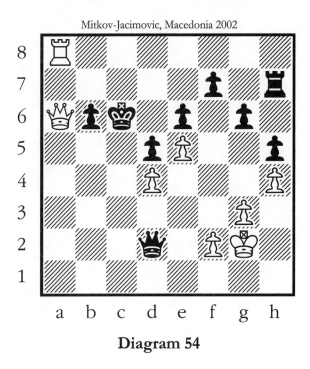

Mitkov-Jacimovic, Macedonia 2002

Diagram 54

Your Solution:

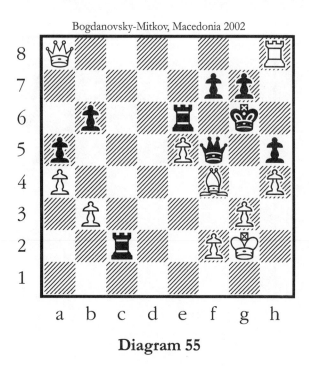

Bogdanovsky-Mitkov, Macedonia 2002

Diagram 55

Your Solution:

MATES IN TWO MOVES

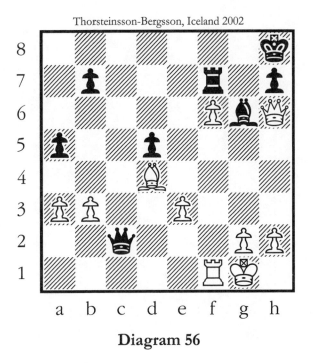

Thorsteinsson-Bergsson, Iceland 2002

Diagram 56

Your Solution:

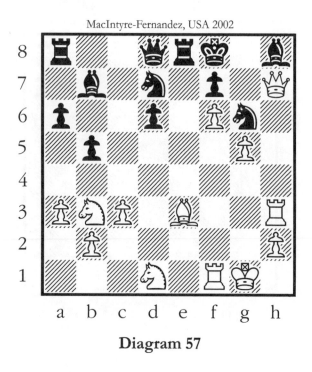

MacIntyre-Fernandez, USA 2002

Diagram 57

Your Solution:

MATES IN TWO MOVES

Velimirovic-Ermenkov, Yugoslavia 2002

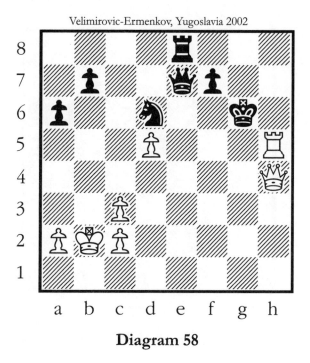

Diagram 58

Your Solution:

Georgiev-Leko, United Arab Emirates 2002

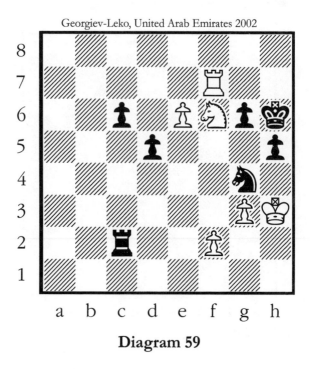

Diagram 59

Your Solution:

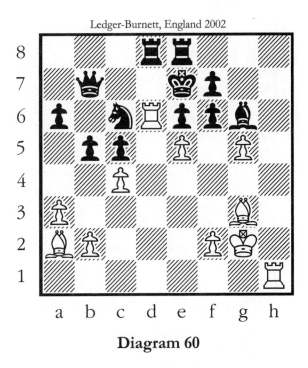

Ledger-Burnett, England 2002

Diagram 60

Your Solution: (look for two ways)

Shredder-Gulko, machine vs. man match 2002

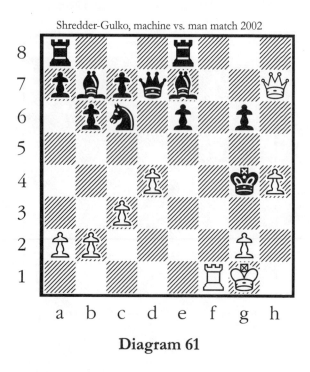

Diagram 61

Your Solution:

MATES IN TWO MOVES

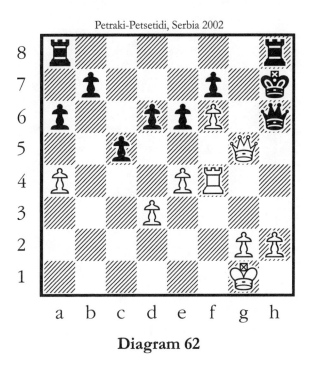

Petraki-Petsetidi, Serbia 2002

Diagram 62

Your Solution:

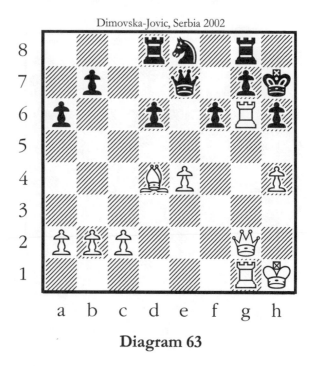

Dimovska-Jovic, Serbia 2002

Diagram 63

Your Solution:

MATES IN TWO MOVES

Handke-Teske, Germany 2002

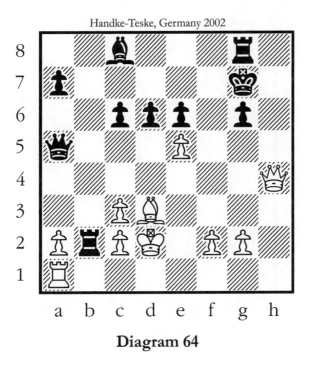

Diagram 64

Your Solution: (look for two ways)

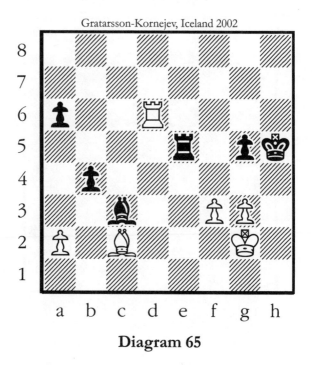

Gratarsson-Kornejev, Iceland 2002

Diagram 65

Your Solution:

MATES IN TWO MOVES

Vogt-Baumgartner, Austria 2002

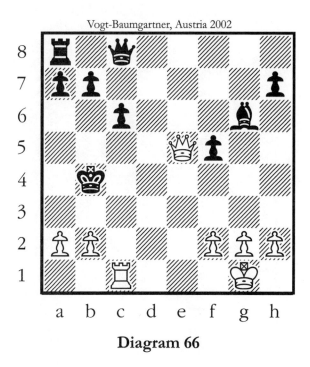

Diagram 66

Your Solution:

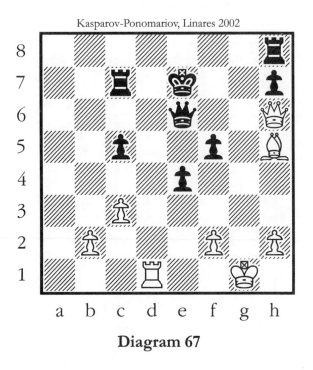

Kasparov-Ponomariov, Linares 2002

Diagram 67

Your Solution:

MATES IN TWO MOVES

Sega-da Silva, Brazil 2002

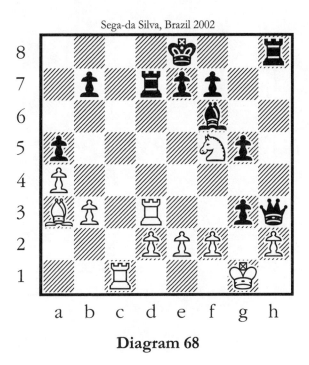

Diagram 68

Your Solution:

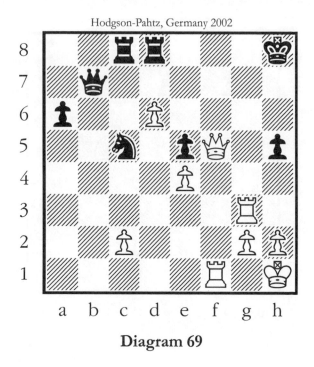

Hodgson-Pahtz, Germany 2002

Diagram 69

Your Solution:

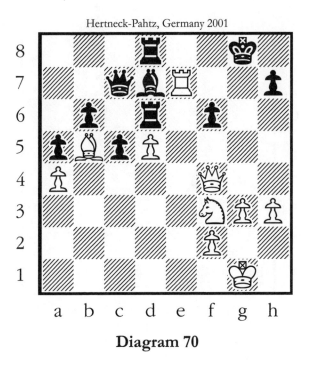

Hertneck-Pahtz, Germany 2001

Diagram 70

Your Solution:

Dchingarov-Mandekic, Croatia 2001

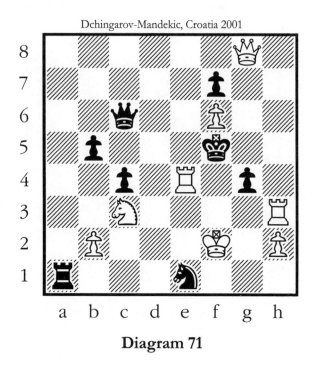

Diagram 71

Your Solution: (look for two ways)

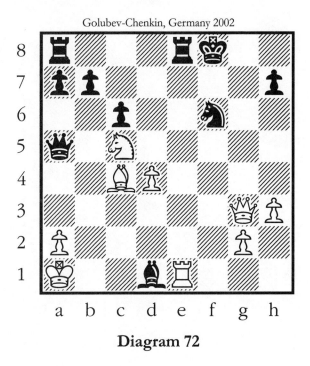

Golubev-Chenkin, Germany 2002

Diagram 72

Your Solution:

Itkis-Manolache, Romania 2002

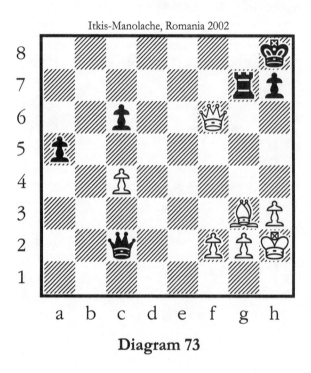

Diagram 73

Your Solution: (look for three ways)

MATES IN TWO MOVES

Bacrot-Van Mil, Switzerland 2001

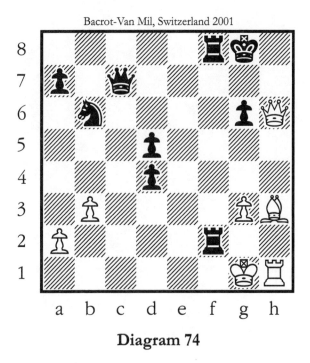

Diagram 74

Your Solution:

Baumgartner-Penz, Austria 2002

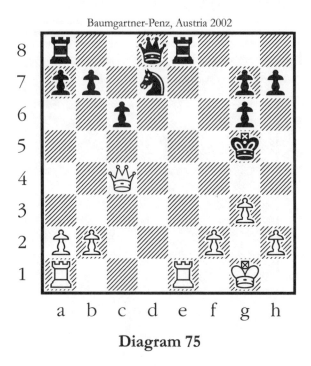

Diagram 75

Your Solution:

MATES IN TWO MOVES

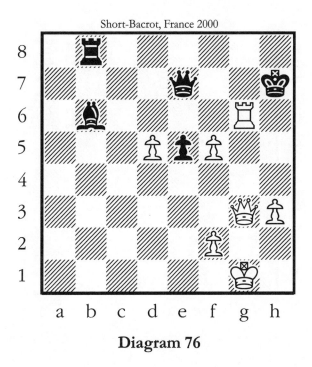

Short-Bacrot, France 2000

Diagram 76

Your Solution:

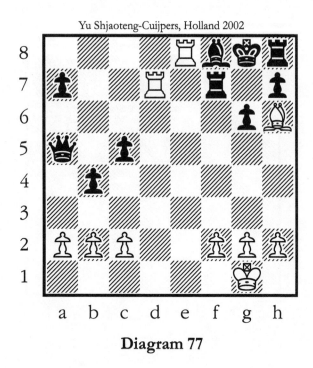

Yu Shjaoteng-Cuijpers, Holland 2002

Diagram 77

Your Solution:

MATES IN TWO MOVES

Dchakaiev-Beschukov, Russia 2002

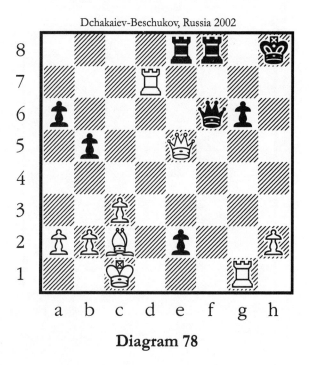

Diagram 78

Your Solution:

Clery-Flament, France 2001

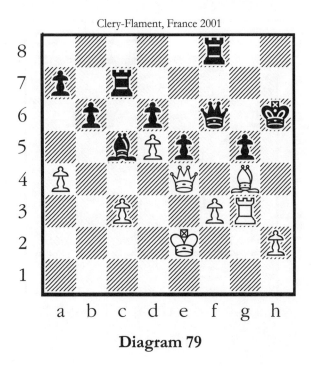

Diagram 79

Your Solution:

MATES IN TWO MOVES

Belov-Pushkov, Russia 2002

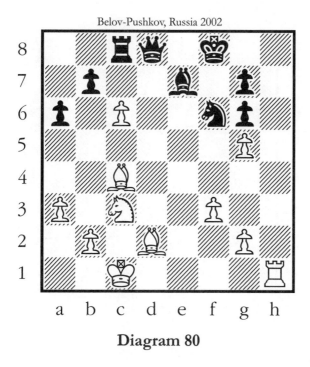

Diagram 80

Your Solution:

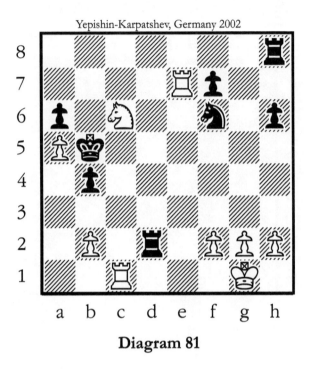

Yepishin-Karpatshev, Germany 2002

Diagram 81

Your Solution:

Gerbelli-Prol, Brazil 2001

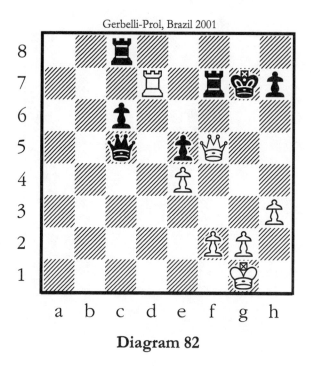

Diagram 82

Your Solution:

Grabarska-Socko, Iceland 2001

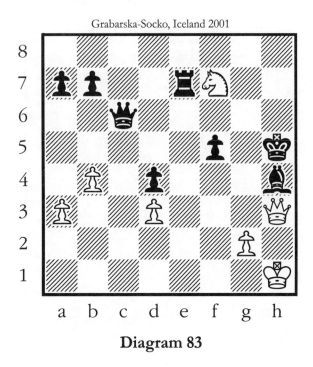

Diagram 83

Your Solution:

MATES IN TWO MOVES

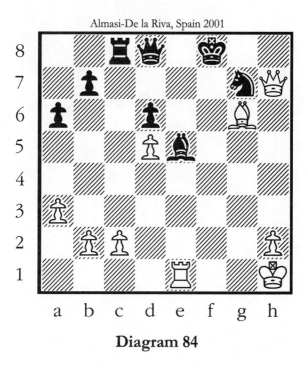

Almasi-De la Riva, Spain 2001

Diagram 84

Your Solution:

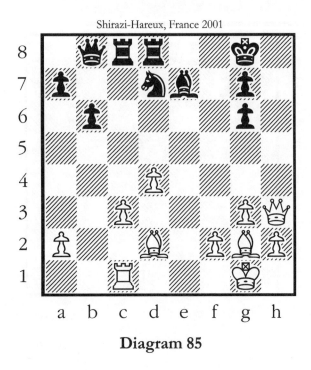

Shirazi-Hareux, France 2001

Diagram 85

Your Solution:

MATES IN TWO MOVES

Geleta-Borsos, Yugoslavia 2002

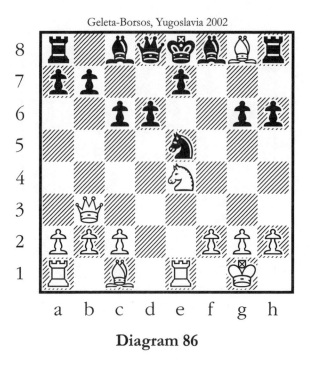

Diagram 86

Your Solution:

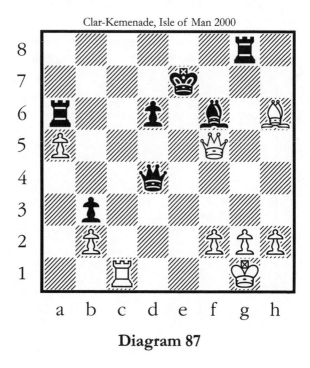

Clar-Kemenade, Isle of Man 2000

Diagram 87

Your Solution:

MATES IN TWO MOVES

Kreiman-Paschall, USA 2002

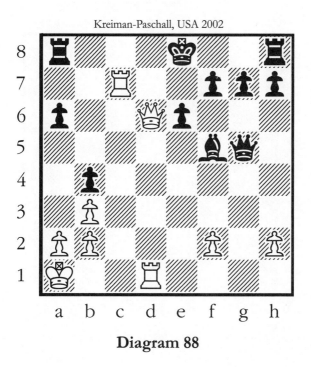

Diagram 88

Your Solution:

Nyysti-Sisatto, Sweden 2002

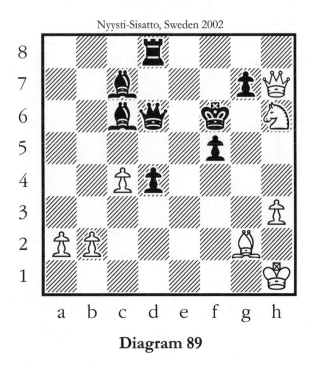

Diagram 89

Your Solution:

MATES IN TWO MOVES

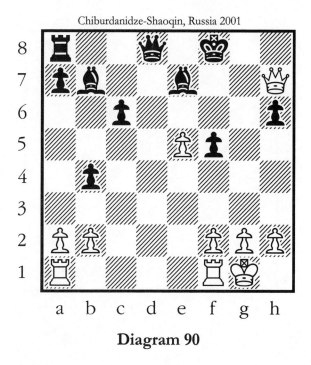

Chiburdanidze-Shaoqin, Russia 2001

Diagram 90

Your Solution:

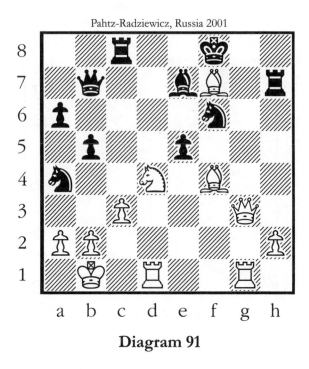

Pahtz-Radziewicz, Russia 2001

Diagram 91

Your Solution:

MATES IN TWO MOVES

Jemelin-Goric, Croatia 2001

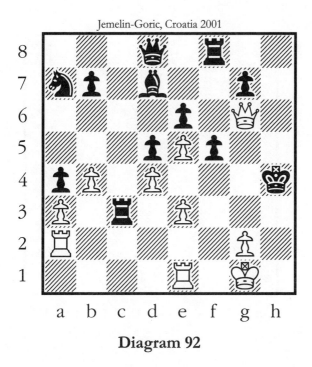

Diagram 92

Your Solution:

Duric-Keele, Croatia 2001

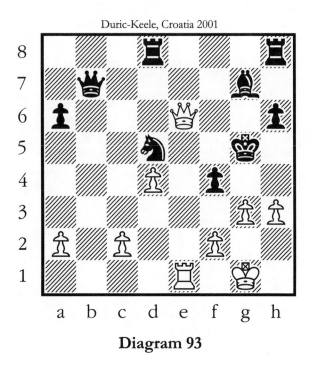

Diagram 93

Your Solution:

MATES IN TWO MOVES

Stefanssen-Heidenfeld, Crete 2001

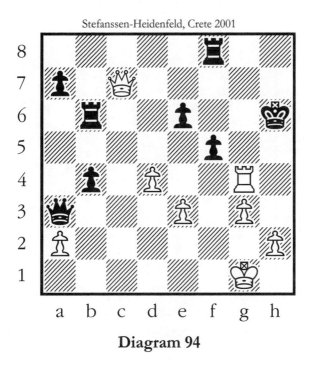

Diagram 94

Your Solution:

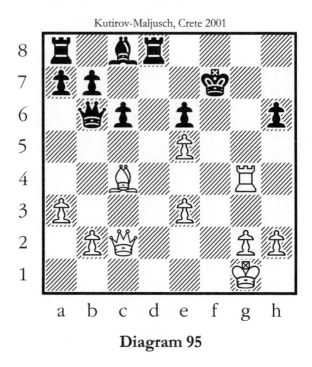

Kutirov-Maljusch, Crete 2001

Diagram 95

Your Solution:

MATES IN TWO MOVES

Milov-Polgar, Russia 2001

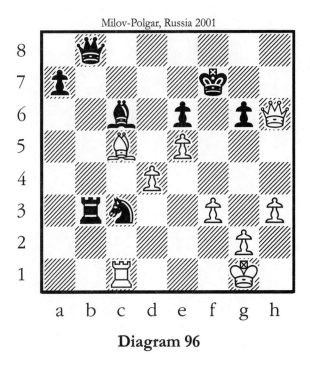

Diagram 96

Your Solution:

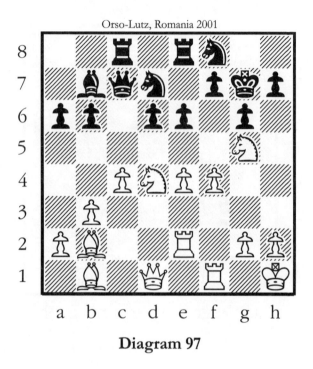

Orso-Lutz, Romania 2001

Diagram 97

Your Solution:

5

A FEW MORE CHALLENGES

As a last challenge, try these three examples. Each one requires more than two moves for mate.

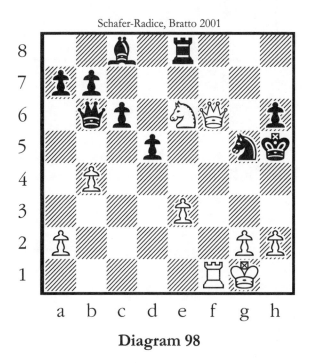

Schafer-Radice, Bratto 2001

Diagram 98

Your Solution: (three moves for mate)

Zambrana-Pina, Cuba 2002

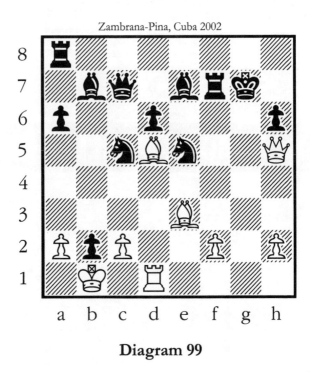

Diagram 99

Your Solution: (four moves for mate)

A FEW MORE CHALLENGES

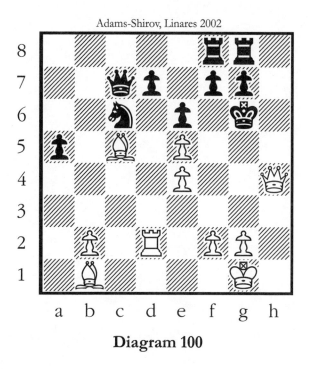

Adams-Shirov, Linares 2002

Diagram 100

Your Solution: (five moves for mate)

SOLUTIONS

6

SOLUTIONS

1.   1. Queen to f6.
The only way to attack the Black king and prevent its escape.

2.   1. Queen to h7 does the trick.
The rook defends the queen from being captured by the Black king.

3.   1. Bishop to f7.
The bishop is backed up by the rook on f1.

4.   1. Queen to f8.
The king has nowhere to flee and nothing to interpose.

5.   1. Rook to h6.
The king is blocked by his own rook.

6.   1. Queen to f8.

The queen is backed up by the bishop, and once again the king's escape route is blocked by its own pawns.

7.   1. Knight to d5.

An unusual predicament where both knights participate in the king's demise.

8.   1. Bishop takes e6.

This simple capture enables both bishops to rake the board.

9.   1. Knight to e8.

The knight now prevents the king from escaping on c7.

10.   1. Rook to g8 or 1. Pawn on h4 to h5.

Either the rook or pawn administers the fatal dose.

11.   1. Queen takes g7.

Snatching this bishop seals Black's fate.

12.   1. Rook takes f8.

The knight can't recapture – it is pinned to the king by the rook on h4.

13.   1. Pawn on e6 goes to e7.

This lowly pawn is guarded by the rook, which in turn is guarded by the bishop on b2.

SOLUTIONS

14.   1. Queen to g7.
The pawn on f6 not only guards the queen, he also prevents the king from escaping to e7.

15.   1. Queen takes g7.
A crude capture ends all resistance.

16.   1. Queen to f8.
The knight controls h7. It's defended by the pawn on h4.

17.   1. Queen to f8 or 1. Queen takes h7.
Sometimes there is more than one way to skin a cat.

18.   1. Queen to h8.
The king's escape is thwarted by the pawn on f4.

19.   1. Bishop takes e6.
The virtue of this capture is that it stops the king from getting to g8.

20.   1. Knight to f6.
The knights do their dirty work despite the absence of White's queen.

21.   1. Knight to c6.
Once again the knight proves its potency.

22.   1. Knight on d6 to f5.
The other knight is needed on e7 to control both g8 and g6.

23.   1. Queen to f5.
The pawn on e3 keeps the king from fleeing to d4.

24.   1. Rook to h3.
Strike while the iron is hot. The queen can't interpose because it is pinned. Why not move the queen to h5 for check? Because Black would move *his* queen to h6!

25.   1. Rook to h5.
There's just one way to administer check, but it's fatal!

26.   1. Bishop to f8.
The king can't take the rook – it's defended by the pawn on f4.

27.   1. Rook to g8.
A lethal combination of rook and bishop.

28.   1. Queen to h8.
In many games an open h-file leads to disaster.

29.   1. Rook to g8.
This rook illustrates the danger of Black's weak back rank.

30.   1. Bishop to f8.
     King to g8.
     2. Bishop to h6.

31.   1. Queen takes g6 – check.
     Rook takes g6.
     2. Knight to f5.

SOLUTIONS

Sometimes it pays to give a little to get a lot. Giving up the queen clears f5 for the final knight thrust.

32.   1. Rook takes h6 – check.
        Pawn on g-file takes h6.
        2. Queen to e5.

The king no longer has any shelter from its pawn.

33.   1. Rook takes f6 – check.
        Pawn on g-file takes f6.
        2. Bishop to h6.
        OR
        1. Rook takes f6 – check.
        Bishop takes f6.
        2. Queen to f7.

The rook can be captured in two ways, each leading to a different mate.

34.   1. Queen takes h7 – check.
        Knight takes h7.
        2. Rook takes h7.

A raw display of brute force along the open h-file. If you don't use it, you lose it!

35.   1. Rook to f5 forces Black's pawn to take f5.
        2. Rook takes f5.

36.   1. Queen takes h7 – check.
        King takes h7.
        2. Rook to h3.

The knight prevents the king from retreating to g8.

37.   1. Rook to h7 – check.
    King takes h7.
    2. Queen to g7.
An old fashioned slam-dunk along the open g-file.

38.   1. Queen to g8 – check.
    Rook takes g8.
    2. Knight to f7.
This is called a "smothered mate," because the king is hemmed in (smothered) by its own forces.

39.   1. Knight on e4 to g3 – check.
    King to g4.
    2. Bishop to f3.
    OR
    1. Knight on e4 to g3 – check.
    King to f6.
    2. Knight on g5 to e4.
Black can choose his own poison.

40.   1. Bishop to d5.
    Pawn on a2 to a1 (becomes a queen).
    2. Bishop to f3.
It's quite rare for a quiet first move to seal Black's fate.
    OR
    1. Bishop to c4.
    Pawn to a1 (becomes a queen).
    2. Bishop to e2.
Again Black perishes along the d1-h5 diagonal.

SOLUTIONS

41.   **1. Pawn on f5 to f6 – check.**
        Bishop takes f6.
        2. Pawn on g-file takes f6.
A pawn provides the final thrust of the dagger.

42.   **1. Queen to g4 – check.**
        King to h6.
        2. Knight to f5.
        OR
        1. Queen to f5 – check.
        King to h6.
        2. Knight to f7.

43.   **1. Rook takes g6 – check.**
        Pawn on h-file takes g6.
        2. Queen to h8.
The rook sac forces open the h-file while the knight prevents an escape to f7.

44.   **1. Knight to e5 – check.**
        King to h8 or to f8.
        2. Knight to g6.
Black has no place to hide.

45.   **1. Queen takes h6 – check.**
        King to g8.
        2 Queen takes g7.
The pawn can't take the queen because it is pinned by the bishop on f6.
        OR
        1. Queen takes h6 – check.

Queen interposes on h2.

2. Bishop takes g7.

46.   1. Bishop to f6 – check.

Knight to g7.

2. Bishop takes g7.

OR

1. Bishop to f6 – check.

Knight takes f6.

2. Knight takes g6.

This time the pawn on h7 is pinned and can't take the knight.

47.   1. Knight to f7 – check.

Rook takes f7.

2. Rook to g8.

The knight is offered in order to ventilate the g-file.

48.   1. Queen takes h5 – check.

King takes h5.

2. Rook to h7.

OR

1. Queen takes h5 – check.

Knight takes h5.

2. Rook on g1 to g6.

OR

1. Queen takes f4 – check.

Pawn on e5 takes f4.

2. Rook on g1 to g6.

In any of these ways, offering the queen deflects the king.

SOLUTIONS

49. **1. Rook to f8 – check.**
> Bishop to g8.

2. Rook takes g8.

White goes straight for the jugular.

50. **1. Rook takes f8 – check.**
> King takes f8 (forced; the rook is pinned).

2. Queen to h8.

Notice how all White's forces join in the attack. Even the innocuous bishop on g5 stops the king from reaching e7.

51. **1. Rook takes h6 – check.**
> King takes h6.

2. Queen to h5.

Another win by pin. The queen can't take the rook because it is illegal to leave g7.

52. **1. Rook to g1 – check.**
> King to f7.

2. Queen to g7.

Once again illustrates the danger once a king has been stripped of its pawns on an open file.

53. **1. Queen to g6 – check.**
> King to h8.

2. Bishop takes f6.

OR

1. Bishop takes pawn on f6 (a quiet move).
> Rook captures bishop on d5.

2. Queen goes to g7 or h8.

Black resigned without waiting.

54.   **1. Rook to c8 – check.**
            King to d7.
        2. Queen to b7.
Straightforward and to the point.

55.   **1. Rook to h6 – check.**
            Pawn on g-file takes h6.
        2. Queen to g8.
The idea is to remove the last pawn sheltering the king.

56.   **1. Queen to f8 – check.**
            Rook takes f8.
        2. Pawn on f6 moves to f7.
The clearance sacrifice of the queen makes the bishop on d4 all-powerful. A slower method is:
        1. Queen to g7 – check.
            Rook takes g7.
        2. Pawn on f6 takes g7 – check.
            King to g8.
        3. Rook to f8.

57.   **1. Queen takes h8 – check.**
            Knight takes h8.
        2. Rook takes h8.
Notice how the pawn on f6 nixes any escape to e7.

58.   **1. Queen to g4 – check.**
            King to f6.
        2. Queen to g5.
The pawn on d5 plays a major role in controlling e6.

SOLUTIONS

59. **1. Knight to g8 – check.**
King to g5.
2. Pawn to f4.
The king can neither advance nor go back.

60. **1. The g-file pawn takes f6 – check.**
King to f8.
2. Rook to h8.
OR
1. The e-file pawn takes f6 – check.
King to f8 (the only defense).
2. Rook to h8.
Once again the rook shows its power on an open file.

61. **1. Queen takes g6 – check.**
King takes h4.
2. Rook to f4.
White sacrificed most of his pieces to exploit the denuded king.

62. **1. Rook to h4.**
Queen takes h4 (what else?)
2. Queen to g7.
The point is to kill the king, not to capture the queen.

63. **1. Rook takes h6 – check.**
King takes h6.
2. Queen to g6.
OR
1. Rook takes h6 – check.
Pawn on g-file takes h6.

2. Queen takes g8.
Without this resource White would be stymied.

64. **1. Queen to f6 – check.**
King to h6 or h7.
2. Rook to h1.
OR
1. Queen to e7 – check.
King to h6 or h8.
2. Rook to h1.
Another cautionary tale of what can happen on an open h-file.

65. **1. Pawn to g4 – check.**
King to h4.
2. Rook to h6.
Nothing fancy. Direct and fatal.

66. **1. Queen to c5 – check.**
King to a4.
2. Pawn to b3 (or Rook to c4).
Danger always lurks after a king strays too far into enemy territory when big guns are still on the board.

67. **1. Queen to g7 – check.**
Queen to f7.
2. Queen takes f7.
The silent rook on d1 plays a critical role in stopping the king from crossing over to the queenside.

SOLUTIONS

68.   1. Rook to c8 – check.
          Rook to d8.
          2. Rook takes d8 (either one).
Point, set, match.

69.   1. Queen takes e5 – check.
          King to h7.
          2. Queen takes h5.
More succinct than:
          1. Queen takes h5 – check.
          Queen to h7.
          2. Queen takes e5 – check.
          Queen to g7.
          3. Queen takes g7.
That sequence would delay mate by one move.

70.   1. Queen to h6.
          Any move.
          2. Queen to g7.
Once again a quiet first move is decisive. A "quiet" move
is one that doesn't contain a capture or a check.

71.   1. Queen to g4 – check.
          King takes f6.
          2. Rook to h6.
          OR
          1. Rook to h5 – check.
          King takes f6.
          2. Queen to g5.
Once again brute forces decides the issue.

72.   **1. Knight to d7 – check.**
        Knight takes d7.
     2. Queen to g8.
Black's knight was compelled to relinquish defense of g8.

73.   **1. Queen to f8 – check.**
        Rook to g8.
     2. Bishop to e5.
     OR
     1. Bishop to e5.
        Queen to g6.
     2. Queen to f8.
     OR
     1. Queen to d8 – check.
        Rook interposes to g8.
     2. Bishop to e5.
Needless to say, Black resigned before White had a chance to exercise any of these options.

74.   **1. Bishop to e6 – check.**
        Rook to f7.
     2. Queen to h8.
Black was forced to block his only escape square on f7 before White could utilize the lethal h-file.

75.   **1. Queen to h4 – check.**
        King to f5.
     2. Queen to f4.
Alas, the king is forced to go where it doesn't want to go.

SOLUTIONS

76.   **1. Rook to h6 – check.**
          King takes h6.
          2. Queen to g6.
This clearance sacrifice sets up a one-two punch.

77.   **1. Rook takes f8 – check.**
          Rook takes f8.
          2. Rook to g7.
The king's path is obstructed by its own men.

78.   **1. Queen to h5 – check.**
          Pawn on g-file to h5.
          2. Rook to h7.
          OR
          1. Queen to h5 – check.
          King to g8.
          2. Queen to h7.
The distant bishop on c2 enforces its will by guarding the rook on h7.

79.   **1. Rook to h3 – check.**
          King to g7.
          2. Queen to h7.
Sometimes "always check, it might be mate" works like a charm.

80.   **1. Rook to h8 – check.**
          Knight to g8.
          2. Rook takes g8.
The same goes for this marauding rook which eats everything in its path.

81. **1. Rook to b7 – check.**
     King to a4.
     2. Rook takes b4.
Nothing fancy, just a brutal massacre.

82. **1. Rook takes f7 – check.**
     King to h6.
     2. Rook takes h7.
     OR
     1. Rook takes f7 – check.
     King to g8 or h8.
     2. Queen takes h7.

83. **1. Queen takes f5 – check.**
     Bishop to g5.
     2. Queen takes g5.
Interposing the bishop merely delays the inevitable.

84. **1. Queen to h8 – check.**
     King to e7.
     2. Queen takes g7.
The bishop can't take the queen because it's pinned by the distant rook on e1.

85. **1. Bishop to d5 – check.**
     King to f8.
     2. Queen to h8.
This typical mating pattern repeats itself in many games.

SOLUTIONS

86.   **1. Knight to f6 – check.**

　　　Pawn on e-file takes f6.

　　2. Queen to f7.

An unusual pin. It's taboo for the knight to take the queen in view of the rook lurking on e1.

87.   **1. Rook to c7 – check.**

　　　King to d8 or e8.

　　2. Queen to d7.

Black has an extra rook, but riches cannot stave off defeat.

88.   **1. Queen to d7 – check.**

　　　King to f8.

　　2. Queen takes f7.

Simple. Direct. Irrefutable.

89.   **1. Queen takes f5 – check.**

　　　King to e7.

　　2. Queen to f7.

The king is trapped in the center of the board.

90.   **1. Pawn to e6.**

　　　Queen to e8 (how else to stop 2. Queen to f7?)

　　2. Queen to h8.

A quiet pawn advance is the only way to force mate.

91.   **1. Bishop to h6 – check.**
> Rook takes h6.
> 2. Queen to g7.

If Black had played King takes f7, White could have mated with Queen to g6. The initial move here is hard to find – yet another example of the power of attack along an open g-file.

92.   **1. Pawn to g3 – check.**
> King to h3.
> 2. Rook to h2.

The king receives no help from its distant couriers.

93.   **1. Pawn to h4 – check.**
> King to h5.
> 2. Queen to f5.

Again a lowly pawn plays a decisive role.

94.   **1. Queen to g7 – check.**
> King to h5.
> 2. Rook to h4 or g5, or Queen to g5 or g6.

All roads lead to Rome.

95.   **1. Queen to h7 – check.**
> King to e8 or f8.
> 2. Rook to g8.

A typical back rank fiasco.

SOLUTIONS

96.   **1. Queen to h7 – check.**
   King to e8.
   2. Queen to e7.
White's bishop guards the queen at its final destination.

97.   **1. Knight to f5 – check.**
   King to g8.
   2. Knight to h6.
White's first move is known as a double check because it also unleashes a threat from the bishop on b2.

98.   **1. Knight to g7 – check.**
   King to h4.
   2. Queen to f2 – check.
   King to g4.
   3. Queen to f4 (or g3).
   OR
   1. Knight to g7 – check.
   King to h4.
   2. Queen takes h6 – check.
   King to g4.
   3. Rook to f4.

99.   **1. Queen takes h6 – check.**
   King to g8.
   2. Rook to g1 – check.
   Knight to g4.
   3. Rook takes g4 – check.
   Bishop to g5.
   4. Rook takes g5.
Black can delay his doom only by interposing pieces in vain. Black saw it coming and resigned first.

100.   **1. Queen to g4 – check.**

King to h6 (Black doesn't play into White's plot with King to h7, so White could play Queen to h5).

2. Bishop to e3 – check.

Pawn to g5.

3. Queen to h4 – check.

King to g6.

4. Queen takes g5 – check.

King to h7.

5. Queen to h6.

Stubborn defense often is overcome by a stubborn attack.

GREAT CARDOZA GAMES BOOKS
POWERFUL BOOKS YOU <u>MUST</u> HAVE

BACKGAMMON FOR WINNERS *by Bill Robertie.* The world's best backgammon player and a two-time champion provides easy-to-understand advice on the basics of playing and winning at backgammon. Ten fast-reading chapters show how to set up a board and move, the opening strategies and replies, middle and end game tactics, basic probabilities, plus back game and doubling strategy. Two sample games are included with move-by-move insights so you learn the winning concepts of play at all stages of the game. A great book for beginning and somewhat experienced players. 192 pages, **$12.95**.

BACKGAMMON FOR SERIOUS PLAYERS *by Bill Robertie.* If you're a backgammon player looking to take your game to the next level, this powerful book from the world's best player will show you how to do it! You'll learn the all-important opening strategies and replies, middle, end and back game techniques, tournament strategies, advanced doubling cube play, and fascinating strategy moves. Includes basic backgammon probabilities and odds, unusual plays, priming strategy, essential bearoff play and more. Features five games by champions with move-by-move insights, 113 diagrams, and the secret dynamics of playing like a champion. 256 pages, **$19.95**.

501 ESSENTIAL BACKGAMMON PROBLEMS *by Bill Robertie.* This is the most detailed guide ever written on essential backgammon strategies. Robertie shows how top players think, plan their strategy from the opening roll, and react to decisive opportunities. 21 chapters cover every part of the game, from the opening roll to the art of endgame settlements. You'll learn when to attack blots, how to master the blitz, about anchors, primes, crunched positions, mastering a race, calculating bearoffs, the back game, checker play problems, doubling decisions, and more. A must-read. 384 pages, **$24.95**.

THE BASICS OF WINNING BRIDGE *by Montgomery Coe.* Learn bridge in one easy reading. From the rules of play, correct bidding techniques and scoring standards, to opening bids and responses, you'll learn how to make bridge a more fun and challenging game. Examples and sample hands throughout. 48 pages, **$4.95**.

HANDBOOK OF WINNING BRIDGE *by Edwin Silberstang.* Easy-reading primer on duplicate and contract bridge is filled with copious examples, illustrations, and anecdotes. You'll learn step-by-step about the rules of play, opening bids and responses, scoring, tournament strategies including the proper evaluation and playing out of hands. Includes coverage of the Jacoby Transfer, Cue, Weak Two, Michael's Cue, Shut-Out, Slam, No-Trump, and advanced, defensive and preemptive bids to important conventions including the Stayman and Blackwood. 176 pages, **$14.95**.

100 BRIDGE PROBLEMS *by Mike Cappelletti.* Cappelletti, a bridge expert and a poker authority, believes that the preferred view to many difficult bridge bidding problems can be determined by applying poker tactics such as intimidation or bluffing at the bridge table. Cappelletti discusses 100 classic bridge problems and recommends an exciting course of action. 224 pages, **$14.95**.

100 BEST SOLITAIRE GAMES *by Sloane Lee & Gabriel Packard.* These are the hundred best and most enjoyable variations of America's most popular card game—solitaire! Loads of examples, diagrams, illustrations, and strategies show you lots of fun ways to enjoy your favorite game. From straight-ahead solitaire to two-player games, Lee makes the game 100 times more fun! 192 pages, **$9.95**.

Order now at 1-800-577-WINS or go online to: www.cardozabooks.com

144